Critical Acclaim for Mad River Rising

"Dana Yeaton's new play is revealed to be a compelling—often funny, sometimes tender—chronicle of a deep personal struggle for identity. . . . Yeaton's characters are very personal and real—and thus powerful. . . . an engaging and moving play."

—*Times Argus*

"*Rising* is a play of universal appeal . . . . It will find a wide audience."

—*The Burlington Free Press*

"*[Mad River Rising]* represents Yeaton's achieved mastery of the medium, a play for all seasons and all locales. The generational tensions that it explores, as well as the cultural prejudices it exposes, have the correct balance between the particular and the general to strike chords of recognition in any audience, much the way *Our Town* has. The play is moving without being either obvious or saccharine. It is also as economical of speech and as dry of wit as the people whom it portrays. . . . It is also an eminently theatrical play, sliding between now and the past and mixing characters of various generations as in a dream."

—*Shelburne News*

Photograph by Sharon Fosbrook

Mae watches over Charlie as Angus lies sleeping.

Mad River Rising

A Play in Two Acts

Dana Yeaton

PenStroke Press
Rochester, Vermont

PenStroke Press
118 Main Street
Rochester, Vermont 05767

PenStroke Press is a student publishing venture established in Rochester High School, in partnership with Inner Traditions International and Schenkman Books, funded by the Randolph Regional School-to-Work Consortium.

Library of Congress Cataloguing-in-Publication Data available
ISBN 0-9669177-2-3

10 9 8 7 6 5 4 3 2 1

Printed and bound in Canada by Webcom

This book was typeset in Garamond
Text design by Erica Andrews, Sarah Blair, and Jenny Jacques
Typesetting and layout by Debra Glogover and Jeanie Levitan
Cover and interior photographs by Sharon Fosbrook
Cover design by Peri Champine

PenStroke Press books are distributed by Schenkman Books, 118 Main Street, Rochester, Vermont 05767 • (802) 767-3702 • schenkma@sover.net

ACKNOWLEDGMENTS

Thanks to the cast that read the first draft of *Mad River Rising* in March, 1997: Herb Propper, Catherine Kenyon, Darri Johnson, Ethan Bowen, and Connan Morrissey. Thanks to my careful readers, Mark Ramont, Bob Small, Don Jordan, Chris Bohjalian, Stephen Kiernan, David Van Vleck, Chuck Meese, and Mark Nash. Thanks for the support of John Kassel, Harry McEnerny, Mike Kiernan, Jeanie Levitan, and Blake Robison. And thanks to Frankie Dunleavy for proofreading, even in her sleep.

Mad River Rising was commissioned with a grant from the Vermont Arts Endowment and was developed and produced as part of The Catherine Filene Shouse New Play Series, which fosters the development of new plays and playwrights for the American theatre and underwrites the development and production of one new play each season at Vermont Stage Company. The Catherine Filene Shouse New Play Series is dedicated to the memory of Mrs. Shouse, a philanthropist and lifelong patron of the arts.

For my father, whom the farm could not keep.

It is impossible to care more or differently for each other than we do for the land.

—Wendell Berry

The photographs in this book are from the production of *Mad River Rising* that premiered at the Royall Tyler Theatre in Burlington, Vermont, on January 13, 1998. It was produced by Vermont Stage Company under the Artistic Direction of Blake Robison. The production was directed by Mark Ramont with scenic design by Jeff Moderegger, lighting design by Matt Richards, costume design by Alan Mosser, and sound design by Timothy W. Nelson. The Stage Manager was Heather E. Skeels.

The cast was as follows:

Angus – Philip Davidson
Charlie – Ethan T. Bowen
Mae/Marie – Tantoo Cardinal
Hopley/Spencer – Mark Nash
Young Angus/Nick – Jonathan Larson

Character List

(for 5 performers)

Angus Stewart: A retired farmer, 77.

Charlie Stewart: Angus' grandson. A management consultant, early 30s.

Mae: A snowshoe-maker of Abenaki and French Canadian descent. She is old.

Young Angus: age 7.

Hopley Stewart: Angus' grandfather, mid 50s.

Marie Cousino Stewart: Angus' daughter-in-law, Mae's daughter, mid 40s *(performed by the actor playing Mae).*

Spencer Eddy: The live-in fiance of Marie's daughter, Cindy, mid 20s *(performed by the actor playing Hopley).*

Nick Stewart: Charlie's son *(performed by the actor playing Young Angus).*

Note on MAE: As much as possible, MAE should appear and disappear, rather than enter and exit. She brings with her a special sound and lighting world which helps delineate time and break scenes.

Time

The present, 1927, and other remembered moments between those dates.

Place

A small town in Vermont.

Setting

The skeleton of an empty hay loft. A temporary post braces up the sagging ridge. The loft door opens out onto a panoramic view of the valley—and a one-story drop. Two or three rusted milk cans are positioned to collect rain. The floor is strewn with loose hay; there is a small stack of bales, behind which actors may be screened from view. Entrance to the main loft is by a wooden ladder coming up through a trap door opening in the floor. A second ladder leads up to the high loft, a small platform tucked up in the gable peak.

ACT I

A match is struck. LIGHTS UP on MAE, lighting her pipe.

MAE. This is the story of Angus Stewart, a man who lived through two great floods. One, when he was just a boy of seven, who went to bed in one world and woke up in another. *(SHE opens the trap door. YOUNG ANGUS shoots up the ladder from below and climbs straight to the high loft.)* The other came when Angus was a man, with a family of his own. It was a flood of machines, of new faces, of progress. It continues today. *(MAE looks down the trap door hole.)* He's a little slower on ladders now.
ANGUS. *(From below.)* I'm comin', goddam it.

ANGUS finally climbs up, in stocking feet, carrying an ax. He looks out at the AUDIENCE.

MAE. You don't say hello, old man.
ANGUS. . . . Vultures. *(Pulls out a whetstone and sharpens his ax.)*
MAE. Angus grew up here in Vermont.

AN AUCTIONEER is heard. ANGUS stops, the AUCTIONEER stops. ANGUS sharpens again, and the cycle repeats. When the AUCTIONEER begins a third time, ANGUS raises his ax.

MAE. I wouldn't do that.

ANGUS chops at the post: Sudden ROAR OF A RIVER AT FLOOD STAGE, LIGHTS dim. ANGUS is confused. He chops again: SILENCE, LIGHTS to normal. ANGUS looks at his ax, impressed.

CHARLIE. *(Calling from below.)* Gramp? . . . Gramp, is that you? *(CHARLIE appears at the top of the ladder—a handsome man dressed for business.)* What the hell are you— *(ANGUS resumes his chopping.)* Gramp you've had us going nuts, people have been look— Where did you go?

ANGUS. . . . Here.

CHARLIE. I— Look, you can't just walk out of that place and go wherever you want. Not tell anyone, you can't just do that.

ANGUS. I did.

CHARLIE. Yeah, and people are going nuts, looking. I'm on my way up to Albany I get a call that you have *disappeared* overnight. Marie's tearing her hair out. No idea where you are.

ANGUS. Shoulda looked here.

CHARLIE. What is that? What are you . . .

ANGUS. It's an ax.

CHARLIE. I mean what are you doing? Isn't that holding something up?

ANGUS. . . . Appears to be.

CHARLIE. Gramp, look, we gotta get you back to the— Where are your shoes? *(Another chop.)* Gramp? Will you stop that! *(Grabs the ax. ANGUS yanks it away.)*

ANGUS. DON'T . . . come within a handle.

CHARLIE. You're threatening me?

ANGUS. I'm reasoning with you. Some stranger's holding an ax, you don't argue with him.

CHARLIE. Gramp it's me, Charlie. . . . Sam's son?

ANGUS. *(Lowering the ax.)* Sam? . . . You came home.

CHARLIE. No, I'm Charlie. Gramp, look, it's time to go back, okay?

ANGUS. Not done yet. *(Resumes chopping.)*

CHARLIE. What are you . . . building?

ANGUS. Vacant lot.

CHARLIE. Gramp, come on. We'll go call Marie.

ANGUS. You go ahead.

CHARLIE. I can't just leave. You might hurt yourself.

ANGUS. Why would I do that?

CHARLIE. Gramp, I'm not leaving you here alone.

ANGUS. Y'always managed in the past, Sam. *(CHARLIE waits. Finally, ANGUS hands him the ax.)*

CHARLIE. Thank you. . . . Look, I'm just gonna make a quick call and be right back. You're not going anywhere, right?

ANGUS. In my stockin' feet?

CHARLIE. Right, well . . . good. *(Starts down.)* Hey, does this place look smaller to you? It looks so small.

ANGUS. . . . Always seemed about this size to me.

CHARLIE. I guess it's different when it's full of hay.

ANGUS. Yeah . . . *(CHARLIE exits.)* there's more hay . . .

ANGUS pulls out a second ax, begins sharpening. AUCTIONEER resumes. ANGUS springs to his feet.

ANGUS. Take 'em all, ya vultures! Go ahead. *(Looks out on an imagined auction.)* Look at you, Stanton Eddy, Myron Farr, Lucien Cousino. Those cows came over with my great great grandfather, does that mean anythin' to you? Slept with 'em on the ship, two heifers and a bull calf. Go ahead, take 'em all. Christly vultures! . . . This time there 'll be nothing left to pick at.

ANGUS raises his ax. A match is struck, AUCTIONEER STOPS. ANGUS turns and sees MAE, lighting her pipe.

MAE. You want to make a vacant lot, Angus, there's a faster way, you know. . . . *(SHE holds up the match. ANGUS reaches for it. She blows it out.)* First, I have something to show you. November 3rd, 1927. Remember? *(MAE conjures the weather with a wave of her hand: SOFT RAIN. LIGHTS dim.)* Last night the skies opened up and haven't stopped. Word comes from the village, part of Main Street washed away. Angus's mother sends him out to calm the animals, "Just talk to 'em, like your grandfather," she says. But Angus is afraid of the cows in the dark, he's only seven. . . . He heads up to the loft where it's safe. *(YOUNG ANGUS climbs up from below and heads to the high loft.)* You don't even say hello to yourself, old man? . . . Next morning, from up in our cabin, my sisters and I look down on the scene below. Instead of a valley, there's an open sea rushing all one way. The bridge is gone, the grist mill, both churches—yours and mine—gone. The Stewart farm looks fine though. The house, barn, silo, tool shed—all the outbuildings—stand as tall and proud as ever. Then we see. The road between the barn and house has turned into a river. The land around the Stewart house is now a shrinking island.

CHARLIE climbs up from below, speaking on a cellphone. FLOOD SOUND fades, LIGHTS come up on ANGUS, cowering. MAE and YOUNG ANGUS have disappeared.

CHARLIE. . . . No, he's here. Where I left him. . . . Gramp, it's for you. . . . Gramp?

ANGUS. Tell her I died.

CHARLIE. It's Marie.

ANGUS. Tell her you found me stone cold hanging from that rafter. . . . You got any matches?

CHARLIE. She says she doesn't want to have to come over here.

ANGUS. Tell her that would be fine.

CHARLIE. Gramp, she wants to talk to you!

ANGUS. I don't speak to strangers.

CHARLIE. She's your daughter-in-law.

ANGUS. No fault of mine.

CHARLIE. What? *(To PHONE.)* Here he is.

ANGUS. *(To PHONE.)* Kinda busy right now Marie, what can I do for you? . . . Yup. . . . Okay. You're the boss. *(Searches the phone and pushes a button.)* Off. *(Hands CHARLIE the phone.)*

CHARLIE. What?

ANGUS. All set.

CHARLIE. All set what?

ANGUS. She's gonna swing by and pick me up.

CHARLIE. Just like that?

ANGUS. Yup. Guess you can go.

CHARLIE. I thought she didn't want to come over.

ANGUS. You think I'd lie about a thing like Marie coming? *(CHARLIE picks up his phone. Dials.)* Go ahead, no sense both of us waiting.

CHARLIE. That's okay . . .

ANGUS. Honest. Don't worry about me. I'm not like those sorry old-timers livin' out at the funeral home . . .

CHARLIE. *(To PHONE.)* Judy, hi. It's Charlie . . .

ANGUS. . . . settin' by the window all day, dreamin' up company.

CHARLIE. Hold on. *(To ANGUS)* Gramp, let me just do this. Business call.

ANGUS. What is it you do?

CHARLIE. Management consultant. *(To PHONE.)* Judy.

ANGUS. Uhuh . . .

CHARLIE. *(To PHONE.)* Yuh, I'm with him now. He's fine, he's— I'll tell ya about it later. Listen, I need you to call Albany for me, see if you can get Michael to bump my presentation to four. . . . I know, what can I do? Just tell 'em family, okay? . . . What's tonight? . . . Oh shit, that's right, I completely— Listen, can I get you to call Karen for me? I know that's weird but I'm not supposed to even talk to her machine till we settle. . . . Thanks, look, just tell her I can't pick up Nick till after 8:00, so he should eat there and—or let's say 8:30, so she can't claim I'm late again. Listen Judy, thanks. . . . May you never go through this. . . . Right, bu-bye. *(Hangs up.)* Gramp, what are you doing?

ANGUS. *(Holds a pair of milk cans high above his head.)*You just watch. *(Lowers the cans until they are straight out at his sides.)* You're next.

CHARLIE. *(Impressed.)* I don't think so.

ANGUS. You could use a little exercise.

CHARLIE. I work out.

ANGUS. Out where? *(Moving a can next to his ear.)* Hello Judy, it's me. Oh wait, I have another call. *(Switching ears.)* Hello? Oh no, I'm too busy with Judy.

CHARLIE. Be careful. You're gonna pull something.

ANGUS. Your turn.

CHARLIE. Uh uh. No way.

ANGUS. Beat by the old man.

CHARLIE. Yeah, well I know what you've been doing all your life. Remember that thing you said: Lift a new born bull every day for a year, you'll be the strongest man on earth.

ANGUS. I never said that.

CHARLIE. You did. And you must have told Dad, because he tried it. With Roosevelt. Wasn't that his name?

ANGUS. Roosevelt . . .

CHARLIE. Yeah, his bull. . . . I think about the day when he couldn't lift him anymore, you know. What that must have been like. . . . Gramp? *(From below, a BULL BELLOWS.)*

ANGUS. Get the ax, Sam.

CHARLIE. What?

ANGUS. He's hangin' there. Get the—

CHARLIE. Gramp! Look, we're gonna go up to the house now.

ANGUS. . . . Not allowed.

CHARLIE. You're not allowed in your own house?

ANGUS. It's Cindy's now.

CHARLIE. Cindy's?

ANGUS. Yeah, Marie's girl. She's got the only key.

CHARLIE. And why is that?

ANGUS. So's she can get in.

CHARLIE. I'm asking why is Cindy living in your house without you?

ANGUS. Well she's got a boyfriend, Sam.

CHARLIE. So the two of them just kick you out.

ANGUS. Three of 'em, countin' Boo. Nice dog.

CHARLIE. Why don't we just go up and talk to Cindy about this right now?

ANGUS. Told ya, not allowed.

CHARLIE. In your own house. See that is just—

ANGUS. She's bad for me anyway, Sam. Paradin' around in her little towel. Hardly eats a thing. You go ahead though.

CHARLIE. No, I'll wait till Marie gets here.

ANGUS. You're gonna get in the pen with *two* Cousino women at once? On purpose? . . . Look, I'm not gonna *chew* my way through that post . . .

CHARLIE. What if I did go up, what would you be doing down here?

ANGUS. Prob'ly take a little nap.

CHARLIE. You must be tired, all that walking.

ANGUS. Actually it's talkin' tires me out.

CHARLIE. Maybe I will just run up, see what Cindy has to say for herself.

ANGUS. Off you go then. *(CHARLIE waits. Finally:)* What? *(ANGUS lies down. CHARLIE takes off his suit coat and covers him.)*

CHARLIE. You get a little rest, maybe you'll start making sense again. . . . Who am I?

ANGUS. What?

CHARLIE. Who am I?

ANGUS. You don't know, I ain't tellin'. *(CHARLIE climbs down. ANGUS reaches under himself and pulls out the ax. SOUND OF RAIN.)* Hey, I didn't even use it yet!

MAE appears; soon after, YOUNG ANGUS can be seen in the loft.

MAE. The new path of the river has eaten away the land from around the Stewart's house, exposing stripes of sand, and stone, and clay. First a crack opens up, then widens and another slice of land falls away and is swallowed by the rushing water. . . . About noon we see your grandfather, Hopley Stewart, go into the barn.

ANGUS. You leave him out of this. *(HOPLEY climbs up from below. He is haggard and wet.)* Grandpa?

HOPLEY calls up to YOUNG ANGUS and points to a rope hanging from a beam. The boy starts down with it, but HOPLEY stops him with a call. He gestures for YOUNG ANGUS to toss it down. HOPLEY exits.

MAE. A little later, Hopley Stewart—

ANGUS. I don't need to hear this. I know this story.

MAE. Ah, but these people don't. Pay attention, old man, you might learn something. . . . His grandfather comes out of the barn tying a rope around his waist. He wraps the other end around a corner post of the tool shed and lowers himself into the river. When he starts toward the stranded house on the other side, that's when we finally understand, my sisters and I—someone is still in the Stewart house.

ANGUS. I'm not listening to this.

MAE. Well you better start, old man. *(Exiting.)* You don't have much time . . .

ANGUS. Just give me those matches. You'll see how much time I need.

The AUCTIONEER's chant drifts up. ANGUS picks up the ax and begins chopping at the post. Suddenly, he stops. He looks up to the loft where HOPLEY now stands, peering down on him.

ANGUS. Two days, Grandpa, they're gonna come, they're gonna auction it off . . . everything that's left. *(HOPLEY climbs down.)* Grandpa, I know it seems wrong but, what if this place was one of us? What if your father or grandfather were lyin' here, broken? Would you leave his body lyin' in plain sight, for the birds and maggots to feed on? Or would you lay it to rest? *(HOPLEY holds out his hand.)* This place should be going to my son, Grandpa. Not to worms.

Defeated, ANGUS hands him the ax. HOPLEY picks up the whetstone. HE strikes it with the ax. A smile breaks across ANGUS' face. HOPLEY drops the ax and stone at Angus' feet and exits. ANGUS slowly picks them up. HE holds the ax and stone over the tinder and strikes. He blows, nursing the sparks.

MARIE. *(From below.)* Angus Stewart, don't you move a God damned inch! *(ANGUS stomps on the tinder and ducks behind the haystack, out of sight.)* I know you're up there, you crazy old coot.

ANGUS. Marie, if you don't mind, I'd like to be alone just now.

MARIE climbs to the top of the ladder. She carries a pair of sneakers.

MARIE. What the hell are you doing behind there?

ANGUS. I'm with a woman just now, and we'd like a little privacy.

MARIE. Four o'clock this morning I get a call from Mrs. Yandow at the retirement home.

ANGUS. It's not her.

MARIE. She tells me that you have disappeared, gone wandering off in the middle of the night, barefoot. Now how do you explain that?

ANGUS. No boots.

MARIE. Look at you. Covered in hay. Sit down. *(Whips off his socks and puts the sneakers on him.)* Foolish man, you about scared me half to death. There I was picturin' you face down in the river, or stuck under a log or— Look at those feet, all scratched up. What're we gonna do with you, chain you up with Boo? . . . Where's Charlie? . . . Angus, where is Charlie?

ANGUS. Charlie who?

MARIE. Don't you play dumb with me, you old codger. Charlie your grandson.

ANGUS. No one here but you, Marie.

MARIE. Then whose spiffy new Pathfinder is that parked up in the drive? With New York plates?

ANGUS. Prob'ly some New Yorker.

MARIE. Why do I even talk to you? *(ANGUS mumbles.)* What?

ANGUS. So I'll keep you in my will.

MARIE. What will? You don't have a will.

ANGUS. 'Course I do. Wrote it up this morning.

MARIE. Oh hush up, you did not.

ANGUS. *(Pulls out a scrap of paper.)* Oops. Forgot to sign. *(Pulls out a pencil and writes. He hands the paper to Marie.)*

MARIE. "Nobody Gets Nothin.'" Well isn't that nice? Honestly.

ANGUS. Needs a witness.

SPENCER. *(From below.)* Marie!

ANGUS. Not Spencer.

MARIE. Up here!

SPENCER. Find him?
ANGUS. No.
MARIE. Yaaas!

SPENCER shoots up the ladder and comes to a sudden stop, staring down on ANGUS.

SPENCER. He looks okay. . . . Can he talk? Last time I seen him he didn't say a word.
MARIE. He doesn't talk much out at the home.
SPENCER. Don't blame him. I'd rather be frickin' dead than live out at that place. . . . Who's the Pathfinder up to the house?
MARIE. That's Charlie. . . . Cindy's cousin.
SPENCER. Figures.
MARIE. Why?
SPENCER. When my Gram was going we had all sorts of new relatives show up.
MARIE. This is different.
SPENCER. Yeah. *(Opens a tin of tobacco. Takes a pinch.)* So y'all set here, 'cause I gotta get back to the shop. *(Offering a pinch to ANGUS.)* Lost a whole morning thanks to you. Next time I'm gonna have t' kick your ass.
MARIE. You put that away. He doesn't need that.
SPENCER. It's good for him.
MARIE. Spencer.
SPENCER. *(Closing the tin.)* If he starts talkin', see if you can find out where those red needle-nose pliers got to. Boo mixed it up with a porcupine last night.

MARIE. Again?

SPENCER. Yeah, he hates those bastards. Don't blame him. There's a couple quills down his throat I can't get at.

MARIE. Spencer, you have got to keep that dumb dog chained up.

SPENCER. Agh, he'll figure it out. . . . Either that or die. *(Tosses the tin to ANGUS. MARIE doesn't notice.)* Cindy gets back tell 'er I got softball tonight. *(Shoots down the ladder.)*

MARIE. Tell 'er yourself!

ANGUS. . . . First thing you have to know to train a dog, is more than the dog.

MARIE. Now why do you do that? Why don't you talk to that boy?

ANGUS. He does enough for both of us. Why Cindy keeps him around I don't know.

MARIE. That is her business. And he thinks the world of you.

ANGUS. Poor judgement.

MARIE. I suppose wanderin' around town in your stockin' feet, middle of the night, that's *good* judgement.

ANGUS. Four o'clock ain't the middle of the night.

MARIE. Angus, what happened? You were doin' so well out there. I saw your little painting ya did. And your new friend, what's his name?

ANGUS. Thief.

MARIE. What?

ANGUS. Turns out he's a thief just like the rest of 'em. First my razor, then my mail starts disappearing. 'S morning I reach for my boots, nothing: I said to hell with it, I'm leavin'.

MARIE. Angus, don't lie to me.

ANGUS. It's true. One day I found my teeth in someone else's mouth.

MARIE. Someone took your boots so you decided to walk six miles in the rain?

ANGUS. I didn't decide it would rain. Plus I come through the woods, not more 'n four miles.

MARIE. And you're telling me this has nothing to do with the fact that you and I were supposed to go to the lawyers tomorrow . . .

ANGUS. Sign it yourself. You don't need me.

MARIE. Angus, you promised. *(CHARLIE starts up the ladder.)* Now who could that be coming up the ladder? Could it—yes it is.

CHARLIE. Man of the hour.

MARIE. Man of the century. Oh my God, Charlie, thank you *so* much for coming. I can't tell you. My heart is still—I feel like I just drank three pots of coffee.

CHARLIE. I'm just glad you called.

MARIE. Believe me, it was pure panic. Panic and luck, because I had your number, I've been trying to get in touch with you and I just thought—

CHARLIE. Yeah I'm sorry about that.

MARIE. Your Uncle Russell says, "Why are you calling someone six and a half hours away?" Two minutes later your secretary calls back and says you'll be here by noon. I could have reached through the phone and kissed that woman.

CHARLIE. Get this . . . Six o'clock this morning I'm sitting on the Tappan Zee Bridge, everything's backed up. I'm just kind of sitting, watching the Southbound lane and it's truck after truck after truck going in, feed the city, right? And I just, right then I go—wonder how Gramp's doin? I'm not kidding.

MARIE. It's a miracle.

ANGUS. Jesus H. Christ.

MARIE. What are you muttering?

ANGUS. Someone thinks about me now it's a miracle.

MARIE. He drove straight up here and *found* you, Angus.

CHARLIE. First place I looked.

ANGUS. He found a farmer in a barn, for cryin' out loud. It's not like he walked across the damn lake.

MARIE. Just don't encourage him.

CHARLIE. Marie, I hate to, but I gotta go.

MARIE. That's impossible. I've already—

CHARLIE. Seriously. I have to be in Albany . . . about an hour and a half ago.

MARIE. Uncle Russell and I are planning on you for dinner.

CHARLIE. Not gonna happen. Really. Next time.

MARIE. Can I at least send you off with some papers to look at?

CHARLIE. Sure . . .

MARIE. Because that's what I've been trying to get in touch about.

CHARLIE. Sorry about that. I've . . .

MARIE. I talked to Karen.

CHARLIE. Well then you know.

MARIE. We didn't really—she just told me you weren't getting your mail, at home.

CHARLIE. Look it's okay. It's not private.

MARIE. Charlie, I am so sorry.

CHARLIE. Hey. Things . . .

MARIE. How's Nick doing, is he . . .

CHARLIE. Nick is I don't know, he's hanging in there. He's tough. Karen says she wants full custody, so . . .

MARIE. What do you want?

CHARLIE. Well, I *want* 50-50, but I work a lot of hours, which doesn't help my case. And I don't particularly want to make a big— ya know? Drag him into this whole mess. . . . Look, I've gotta— Where are these papers you want me to look at?

MARIE. Charlie, you should stay.

CHARLIE. I can't. I'm already— It's not good.

MARIE. . . . They're in the car. Let me just grab them.

CHARLIE. What's this all about?

MARIE. My new calling. I'm a, a non-profit entrepreneur.

CHARLIE. You're starting a business?

ANGUS. Stealing, more like it.

CHARLIE. What?

MARIE. Don't listen to him. Just let me grab this stuff, I'll be right back. I'm sure you'll understand it all much better than I do. *(Exits down ladder.)*

CHARLIE. Gramp, what's going on?

ANGUS. Like you don't know.

CHARLIE. What are these papers she's talking about?

ANGUS. They're *her* problem now. I signed everything over to her.

CHARLIE. The farm?

ANGUS. The whole Christly mess.

CHARLIE. To her? Not to Russell?

ANGUS. Doesn't go to the second son, Sam, goes to the first. Only you said no. You don't get to make up how things work.

CHARLIE. So you give it to the daughter-in-law? That's how it works?

ANGUS. You know what they do? Her and her daughter, you know that big oven, up in the kitchen? The bread oven? I was born in that oven, d'ju know that? *(HOPLEY appears in the high loft. HE is dry, healthy looking. CHARLIE doesn't notice him.)* Came out of my mother blue, they figured I was cold, so they popped me in the oven to warm me up. 'Course, I was the runt. I was smaller than my sister and she was a year and a half younger. Whenever I couldn't reach something or couldn't throw the harness over the team, my grandfather'd tell me I was going back in the oven to rise. . . . Know what she uses that stove for now? Burnin' junk mail.

CHARLIE. Gramp, what exactly was it you signed?

ANGUS. Ashes driftin' all over the place.

CHARLIE. You can't just throw away what was given to you.

ANGUS. Nothing was *given* to me, mister. See, that's your problem. No one gives you land. You earn it, over time—

CHARLIE. You know what I mean.

ANGUS. —over a lifetime. Not yours, your father's. You watch, you work and later on, you provide for the needs of the father. That's the promise. And the deed is not passed on until *he* has passed on. Which is why this place can never be yours.

MARIE. *(Climbs up, carrying a stack of folders. HOPLEY disappears.)* I'm just gonna show you these real quick 'cause I know you have to go, but I was thinking that some of the more important things, you can follow me over to the school on your way out and we can get copies. . . . Like these are the letters of support. In-kind contributions. . . . These are just notes. All my notes. Here's the land trust agreement which . . .

CHARLIE. Wait wait. What is all this?

MARIE. Well hold on. Because here is my big coup. Look.

CHARLIE. "Letter of Intent."

MARIE. From our anonymous donor.

CHARLIE. Who's that?

MARIE. Well it's anonymous, silly. But look.

CHARLIE. "One hundred and twenty eight thousand dollars." What is this for?

MARIE. . . . You really haven't been getting your mail.

CHARLIE. No.

MARIE. We have a closing tomorrow at ten.

CHARLIE. What?

MARIE. We're putting the land in a trust, which means we sell off the development rights, but we keep the property.

CHARLIE. I know what it means. Why?

MARIE. It was either that or lose the place.

CHARLIE. I mean, what happened?

MARIE. Ask Mr. Independence over there, he kept assuring me. Taxes paid? "Yup." Mortgage paid? "Yup" Utilities? Creditors? "Yup. Yup." . . . One afternoon the electricity's cut off and Cindy tries to use the cookstove, we end up with the Fire Department over here. They later determine the cause of the blaze was about 14 months worth of unopened mail stashed up the stove pipe. . . . Look at him over there, in his own world.

CHARLIE. He can hear you, Marie.

MARIE. 'Course he can. Doesn't mean he listens. . . . Close your mouth there, Angus, you're gonna be drooling on your clean shirt. . . . I gotta get him back. He's ready for a nap.

CHARLIE. Hold on, I just want to get straight on—

MARIE. Just look over that agreement will you? Call me tonight. If we need little changes, fine. There's a number in there for the lawyer, who I got for nothing by the way.

CHARLIE. What happens to him? *(Indicating ANGUS.)*

MARIE. I'm taking him now.

CHARLIE. I mean long-term.

MARIE. Nothing. No change. . . . What?

CHARLIE. Maybe we should go outside.

MARIE. Angus knows what's going on. . . . Charlie, what?

CHARLIE. I don't want him being there, at the home. I feel like he's— I mean look at him.

MARIE. He's 77 years old, he's not supposed to look good.

CHARLIE. He doesn't even know who I am, Marie. He thinks I'm Dad.

MARIE. When's the last time you were up?

CHARLIE. Last summer I was here. And I send a card, birthday cards. . . . You should have seen him when I got here. He was *alive,* there was sweat on his face, he looked— He had those milk cans up in the air like, like a marine.

MARIE. He has his good spells.

CHARLIE. I just picture him out at the home with like tapioca pudding on his chin and someone reaches over and . . .

MARIE. I bet he'd like to see more of his grandson, which would be a help to me, because right now I'm *it.* Russell he won't see and your dad doesn't want to know.

CHARLIE. That's not true.

MARIE. I don't *want* to be the only person in his life, you know.

CHARLIE. What about Cindy?

MARIE. She was taking care of him right along there, until it just became obvious . . .

CHARLIE. So he gets moved out and she gets the key to the house.

MARIE. I don't like the sound of that.

CHARLIE. Marie, I don't want him going back to that nursing home.

MARIE. Well he can't live alone.

CHARLIE. Then we get a little help.

MARIE. It's beyond that.

CHARLIE. Then we get a lot of help! Do you know who that man is? Do you know what he has done, what he has witnessed? This is *his* property, the Stewart farm—

MARIE. Then where are all the Stewarts?

CHARLIE. I'm here!

MARIE. For a day. . . . Angus come on, get up.

CHARLIE. Gramp, if you want to stay with me, you can.

ANGUS. She's my boss.

CHARLIE. You are your own boss.

MARIE. Angus has appointed me his guardian.

CHARLIE. What?

MARIE. It was a voluntary agreement. Which I would be happy to discuss with you later.

CHARLIE. Voluntary.

MARIE. Yes.

CHARLIE. Which means he can voluntarily break it.

ANGUS. I can?

CHARLIE. Of course. And she knows that.

MARIE. Don't do this Charlie.

CHARLIE. Don't what? Don't ruin your real estate plans?

MARIE. You cannot talk to me that way.

CHARLIE. My father grew up on this farm.

MARIE. So did my husband. So did this hay. So what?

CHARLIE. It should stay in the family.

MARIE. That is what I have been trying to *do* for the past six months. And that is exactly what you are jeopardizing by your stupid . . . interference.

CHARLIE. This is my life too, Marie. How can I be interfering in my own life?

MARIE. Why don't you ask your wife that question? Or your son, next time you run into him?

CHARLIE. This has nothing to do with them. This is about Angus and what we are willing to do to make sure he lives out his days with dignity.

MARIE. Like going to court? Like being declared incompetent? Because that's the alternative, Charlie. That was where Russell was headed when I stepped in. It's not exactly my dream to have a 77-year-old child on my hands.

CHARLIE. Then don't.

MARIE. I am not going to watch this thing fall apart, Charlie. Either he comes with me, right now, or I am going to my lawyer and start proceedings to have him declared incompetent. And that will be a true indignity.

CHARLIE. *(Looks at ANGUS. Pause.)* Just give me a few minutes, okay? . . . I'll take him back myself.

MARIE. . . . He'll need to eat. *(Exits.)*

ANGUS. Well . . . guess you told her. *(No response from CHARLIE. ANGUS offers him some chew.)*

CHARLIE. What are you doing? You're not supposed to have that.

ANGUS. As a matter of fact, I am. It's my antidote.

CHARLIE. For what?

ANGUS. My woman pills.

CHARLIE. What?

ANGUS. They're turning me into a woman.

CHARLIE. What are you talking about?

ANGUS. Just what I said. They got me on estrogen. Turning me into a woman.

CHARLIE. . . . It's not working.

ANGUS. That's 'cause of the chew. D'ju ever see a woman chew? . . . Go ahead. Won't hurt ya.

CHARLIE. I have to make a couple calls . . . then we'll go.

ANGUS. What is it again you do for work?

CHARLIE. Management consultant.

ANGUS. What's one of them do?

CHARLIE. We advise people how to manage their business.

ANGUS. Hmmm . . . Guess Marie would be a good one of those, huh? *(CHARLIE picks up the phone.)* I don't suppose you get a lot of French Cannuck women out in California . . .

CHARLIE. I don't live in California. That's Dad.

ANGUS. Well I'm gonna let you in on a little secret. Next time you find yourself tanglin' with a Cannuck woman, the word is "yup." 'Specially if she's got Indian blood in her like Marie. Any other word's a waste, just yup, yup, yup, till she goes away. Then you do whatever you damn please. *(CHARLIE dials. ANGUS starts up the ladder to the high loft.)*

CHARLIE. Where are you going?

ANGUS. Didn't you ever swing off 'o that rope into the hay?

CHARLIE. *(Springing to his feet.)* There's no hay! . . . Stop. What are you trying to— Angus you stop or we are leaving right now. I'm serious.

ANGUS. You know if I had a mother, you'd remind me of 'er.

CHARLIE. Angus. Stop right where you are. Do you understand?

ANGUS. *(Continuing up.)* Yup.

CHARLIE. Stop it! . . . Stop! *(HE grabs ANGUS by the ankle, and is instantly kicked in the mouth. Long pause.)* I'm not going to fight you, Angus.

ANGUS. Then you ain't gonna win.

CHARLIE. We are on the same side. We want the same thing.

During the following, HOPLEY appears in the high loft. HE looks down on Angus.

ANGUS. If that was true, we wouldn't have a problem would we, Sam? I'd be living up to the house, you'd have your own place over on the knoll. Whatever time you got up in the morning, I'd get up ten minutes earlier, so's I could watch you walk to work. Your boy comin' right behind, trying to step in your bootprints. . . . Now if you'd wanted that too, this place would be full to the rafters with hay, wouldn't it? . . . 'Stead of dust.

CHARLIE. Gramp, what happened is no one's fault. It's everywhere. It's an economic reality.

ANGUS. You ever read the Bible, Sam?

CHARLIE. No.

ANGUS. But you believe in God.

CHARLIE. I'm not sure.

ANGUS. Well let me tell you a little economic reality. You got your Old Testament and your New Testament—vengeful God, loving God. And you've got to invest everything you're worth in one or the other, right? Go with the old one. He never lets you down.

ANGUS looks up to HOPLEY, who turns and exits. CHARLIE turns away and dials. MAE appears.

MAE. No one living had ever seen rain so hard for so long.

ANGUS. You can save your breath, Mae, I don't need your matches. The minute I get rid of this fella I'll have this place up in flames.

MAE. What makes you think he'll go?

ANGUS. You don't know much about boys, do ya.

MAE. I know about you. *(FLOOD SOUND. ANGUS looks up at YOUNG ANGUS, who peers out the high loft window.)* Hopley Stewart is just a few steps into the water when his feet are swept from under him. On the opposite shore, Angus' mother and sister watch as the old man skips along the top of the water like a cork on a fish line. "You think it's so funny," my mother says to me, "you go down and help." I don't argue, but I don't run. By the time I arrive, Hopley's already hauled himself back to the near shore and is headed for the barn.

Next thing I know we're piling the ox-cart with stones, steel tools, tree stumps, anything to weigh it down for the old man's next attempt to cross. When the cart can hold no more, Hopley tells me go find you in the barn. "Tell him go check on the heifers," he calls out. Then he climbs onto the backs of his oxen and begins that chant of his, the one that made them pull.

From offstage, we hear Hopley's chant. ANGUS tries to join in as YOUNG ANGUS and MAE exit.

CHARLIE. *(On the cell phone, leaving a message.)* Michael. Charlie Stewart, calling from deepest Vermont, listen thanks a lot for switching things around, I appreciate it. Judy said you can fit me in at *six,* that's great, look I'm wondering though—I'm supposed to be back in the city by 8:30—is there any chance—see I need to be *leaving* Albany at six—any chance we could do 5:15? 'Cause I can pitch this thing in 45 minutes if I have to. *(CHARLIE glares at ANGUS, who continues to practice his call.)* Sorry to be messing you around like this, I guess Judy told you *some.* Anyway, if I don't hear from you I'll get myself there by five and just hope for the best. See you then, thanks bye. *(HE hangs up. ANGUS stops.)* . . . You only sing when I'm on the phone?

ANGUS. Didn't want to eavesdrop.

CHARLIE. Do me a favor, will you? *(Dialing.)* This next call, eavesdrop very attentively. *(To PHONE.)* Hello, this is

Charlie Stewart again. I'd like to speak to Doctor Proxmire please. . . . Well, I just spoke with someone at the Home Health Service and apparently they need a call from his physician before they can send someone over today . . .

ANGUS. What?

CHARLIE. Well this *is* urgent. . . . I don't know, meals? Light cleaning maybe? We'll have to sort of assess—hey! *(ANGUS has grabbed the phone from CHARLIE.)* Angus, what are you doing? *(ANGUS walks to the ladder and holds the phone over the opening.)* Angus, please give me the— *(ANGUS drops, then catches it.)* NO!

ANGUS. You really love this little thing, don't ya?

CHARLIE. There's someone on the other end right now.

ANGUS. You think the fall would hurt her?

CHARLIE. Just let me hang up, and we'll talk.

ANGUS. I don't want to talk.

CHARLIE. Okay, we won't talk! *(Pause.)*

ANGUS. Actually, it's okay if *I* talk. I just don't want *you* to talk. *(CHARLIE consents. ANGUS takes in the silence.)* Hear that? . . . That is the sound of no one telling me what I should do for my own good. . . . Mmmm. *(To PHONE.)* Hello this is Angus Stewart. I have a message for Dr. Proxmire. . . . Tell him I died and I want my money back. *(Pushing a button.)* Off. *(Beat.)*

CHARLIE. All right Angus—

ANGUS. Uh uh . . . *(ANGUS is threatening to drop the phone down the opening.)* Got a simple question for you, Sam.

Answer it truthfully, we can spare your precious little friend here. Understand? *(CHARLIE nods.)* Why did you come back?

CHARLIE. . . . To help. *(ANGUS drops the phone down the opening.)* Jesus!

ANGUS. *(Peering down.)* They don't make those things very solid do they?

CHARLIE. I was telling the truth!

ANGUS. You want to help me.

CHARLIE. Yes.

ANGUS. You gonna pay my bills?

CHARLIE. No.

ANGUS. You gonna get my cows back? Maybe you can fix my roof.

CHARLIE. How about keeping you here? On the farm. Isn't that worth something to you?

ANGUS. I'm already here.

CHARLIE. And what about Marie?

ANGUS. She's not here.

CHARLIE. You think she's going to let you just live in the barn?

ANGUS. Why not? Your relatives over in Scotland did.

CHARLIE. That's not true.

ANGUS. 'Course it is, all over Europe. People upstairs. Livestock down. That way you can keep an eye out. Plus you get the heat rising . . .

CHARLIE. *(Picks up Marie's folders.)* Have you looked through this?

ANGUS. Don't need to.

CHARLIE. But you know what it is, right? . . . It's a way to hang on to the farm.

ANGUS. What farm? You smell a farm here? You see anyone out there plowin', harrowin'. You see any boys out there tossin' bales?

CHARLIE. Gramp, it's a trust. You keep the land. You do what you want, you have animals. All they do is buy your development rights.

ANGUS. And why do you suppose they do that, huh? Pitch in, help a neighbor? No, they want to live in a goddam postcard. They think it might be nice to live next to the past.

CHARLIE. But if they're willing to pay—

ANGUS. Land is not for lookin' at, mister. It's for workin'.

CHARLIE. So what's your solution?

ANGUS. You don't want to know.

CHARLIE. Gramp I don't care what you do. As long as *you're* the one deciding.

ANGUS. And you're gonna help?

CHARLIE. Yes. If I can . . .

ANGUS. Nah, you wouldn't do it.

CHARLIE. Try me.

ANGUS. Put it back.

CHARLIE. Put what back?

ANGUS. Level every building, fell every tree, pick every goddam stone off every wall, and fling 'em back in the fields where the floods and glaciers left 'em. . . . You don't seem to like my idea.

CHARLIE. I don't think—

ANGUS. You know what they want? They want a "nature trail." Down along the intervale, a "riverside walkway." D'ju know that?

CHARLIE. These things can be negotiated.

ANGUS. With Marie?

CHARLIE. Yes and with the other involved parties who—

ANGUS. I seen you negotiate with Marie. . . . Tell ya a secret: you don't dicker with someone till you know what they're after and d'ya know what that means? You don't dicker with women. And you sure as hell don't dicker with a woman's got Indian blood.

CHARLIE. What are you talking about?

ANGUS. She can't help it, Sam, we're the settlers. She wants her land back, she don't want to negotiate. She wants revenge. She already stuck me out there on the goddam reservation! . . . You go ahead and laugh, but you see if she doesn't get her way.

CHARLIE. No I just— Gramp, look. According to this, she doesn't get anything. It all stays in your name.

ANGUS. And look who's got my name! Huh? You look at the bottom of that sales agreement. "Signing for Angus Stewart." My name ain't Marie Cousino Stewart.

CHARLIE. Gramp, there is a lot of good in this agreement.

ANGUS. Then go sign it with her. Go be a witness. Just go. I'm tired. *(ANGUS lies in the hay.)*

CHARLIE. I don't want you to just quit.

ANGUS. Well maybe it's time I do. That's one thing we've never been very good at in this family. Knowin' when to get out. 1986, could've gone for Whole Herd Buy-out, could've taken my government check and headed down to Florida. . . . Two years later, when I had no choice, there was barely a herd to auction. But Stewarts tend to keep going, beatin' those dead horses like they're gonna come back to life.

CHARLIE. Is that what I need to do?

ANGUS. Hmmm?

CHARLIE. Beat you back to life?

ANGUS. You're kind of a . . . annoying little shit aren't ya?

ANGUS turns over to sleep. CHARLIE exits. ANGUS picks up the ax and stone. MAE appears, heading for the high loft.

MAE. He'll be back before you can even get that started.

ANGUS. Don't bet on it.

MAE. He's as stubborn as you, old man. If he's not back in five minutes I'll torch the place myself.

ANGUS. Now that I would enjoy, watching you burn down your daughter's barn.

MAE. It's your barn, Angus, not hers. Anyway, I won't have to, because he'll be back. And you'll be glad. Just like you were the first time I appeared in your loft.

ANGUS. Oh Jesus. Another installment.

FLOOD SOUND rises. YOUNG ANGUS and MAE look out the window.

MAE. I've just climbed up next to young Angus in the loft, when we see the tool shed start sliding down the bank.

The moment it touches the water, it turns and shoots straight for the team. Hopley is struck in the shoulder and the oxen are knocked off their feet. The old man clings to the yoke and just manages to pull the pin, freeing the animals from each other. . . . A few moments later, one of the oxen reemerges on the near shore. The other, along with your grandfather and the cart, is already out of sight.

MAE covers YOUNG ANGUS with her shawl. He smells it, and hands it back. MAE exits.

CHARLIE is now typing on a laptop computer. He reads one of Marie's documents, checks his watch, takes a bite of a left-over Egg McMuffin, returns to his typing. He is in business mode. CHARLIE picks up the broken cell phone—the flip-down mouthpiece dangles by a wire. He connects a cable from his laptop to the phone. CHARLIE looks at Angus, then types a few commands on the laptop. We hear the high-pitched tones of a FAX CONNECTION.

CHARLIE stands and stretches his stiff neck. He looks at the milk cans, goes to them. He checks that Angus is asleep, then lifts the cans into the air. He slowly lowers them, until they are out at his sides. Suddenly his neck goes into spasm. The cans crash to the floor. ANGUS sits bolt upright.

ANGUS. Roosevelt! *(Panicked, disoriented.)* He's hanging, Sam! Get the ax!

CHARLIE. It's okay.

ANGUS. The bull is hanging by his chain. . . . Roosevelt!

CHARLIE. Easy.

ANGUS. Floor just gave way under him. Just hangin' there. . . . Did you chop the post?

CHARLIE. Yes. It's okay.

ANGUS. Should have sharpened the ax.

CHARLIE. It's okay.

ANGUS. And you're still here?

CHARLIE. 'Course I am.

ANGUS. He got ya though, didn't he? *(Touching Charlie's lip.)* All swelled up.

CHARLIE. It's nothing. I'm fine. . . . Come sit down.

ANGUS. Gotta sharpen that damn ax, Sam.

CHARLIE. We will. *(Pause.)* Feeling better?

ANGUS. I'm fine.

CHARLIE. Thought you might be hungry.

ANGUS. No.

CHARLIE. Got some tasty left-overs here.

ANGUS. That's a paper bag.

CHARLIE. Go ahead. Little grade-A American beef . . . or Argentinian maybe. Gramp listen, I uh—

ANGUS. D'ju hear about over in England? Mad cows.

CHARLIE. Yeah.

ANGUS. Don't blame 'em . . .

CHARLIE. Gramp we've got to make some plans, okay? For the next day or two. And then we can think about the long-term.

ANGUS. Been thinkin' the same thing.

CHARLIE. Really? What?

ANGUS. . . . Why don't we hear yours first?

CHARLIE. Okay, well, I just want to describe a possible plan. I'm not trying to persuade you, or tell you what to do . . .

ANGUS. That's what Marie's for.

CHARLIE. Uh, not anymore.

ANGUS. What?

CHARLIE. Think about Marie's plan, without Marie.

ANGUS. No Marie?

CHARLIE. Right. Property is yours, free and clear, you're livin' at home, doin' what you want—but there is no more Marie.

ANGUS. *(Devastated.)* Marie died?

CHARLIE. No, Gramp. I just . . . you okay?

ANGUS. No, I'm fine. I'm . . . You won't tell her I was . . .

CHARLIE. No no. . . . Come look at this. *(CHARLIE leads ANGUS to the computer.)*

ANGUS. Nice little machine. Probably just about do your taxes for ya, won't it?

CHARLIE. Actually, yeah. Pretty much my whole *life* in there.

ANGUS. "Microsoft Works."

CHARLIE. Here.

ANGUS. "VOLUNTARY GUARDIANSHIP." *(CHARLIE signals to go on.)* "PETITION FOR TERMINATION OF AGREEMENT." . . . You fired the boss? *(CHARLIE cursors to the bottom.)* *I* fired the boss . . . Has she seen this?

CHARLIE. Don't know, I doubt it. But your lawyer has, I just faxed it to her. *(ANGUS starts to cover the computer with hay.)* Stop it. What are you doing?

ANGUS. That's *her* lawyer too!

CHARLIE. Stop it.

ANGUS. She's going to have me declared incontinent!

CHARLIE. Actually she's not.

ANGUS. She said—

CHARLIE. First of all, she can't have you declared anything that you are not. Okay?

ANGUS. . . . Like if she declared me rich.

CHARLIE. Right. Only we don't have to worry about Marie any more, okay? Tomorrow morning, ten o'clock, you and I are going to the closing without Marie. Okay? . . . Angus?

ANGUS. I see what's happening here. . . . You're taking her job.

CHARLIE. No. That is the last— I'm just there to look things over. You're the one who signs.

ANGUS. I'm the boss.

CHARLIE. You are the boss.

ANGUS. So you'll be there.

CHARLIE. I will be there and Marie will not. *(Disconnecting the phone.)* I've just got to do some juggling.

ANGUS. You ever had about 800 pounds of angry animal slip a horn up under your belt, fling you through the air and you're lying on your back, breath knocked out of you, she's about to bring her hooves down on your head?

CHARLIE. That's what Marie's gonna do to me?
ANGUS. No. Just asking . . .

MAE appears. During the following, ANGUS is using a pitchfork to shape two mounds of hay. CHARLIE tries to fix the phone.

MAE. You insult my daughter, you think I'll leave, old man? Is that it? . . . Marie is no cow.
ANGUS. I compare a human to a cow, it's the not the human I'm insulting. . . . Marie's all right. She's just a little too much like you.
MAE. You just have to do what we want and we go away. . . . I notice you haven't torched the place yet. Did you change your mind?
ANGUS. Thought we might spend one last night up here.
MAE. You're goin' soft, old man. . . . Been a while since you and I stayed up here, no? *(FLOOD SOUND up. YOUNG ANGUS appears in the high loft.)* We look across the valley and see headlights moving up and down the hill, like ants. Later, we find out they moved the library up to Jewett's store. Every single book.
ANGUS. Next morning, Jewett's washed away.
MAE. And your farm house, just a hundred feet away, seems like it's on the other side of the ocean. *(Lantern light shines in through the high loft window.)* From up here, we can make out the silhouette of your mother up in her bedroom, sewing by the light of a lantern. Now and then your sister looks out . . . *(YOUNG ANGUS waves,*

gets no response, stops.) but she can't see us in the dark. Downstairs, the animals are strangely quiet.

MAE exits. ANGUS tosses the pitchfork into the haystack. CHARLIE is trying to fix the phone.

ANGUS. I was trying to remember, Sam, if you and I ever spent a night up here.

CHARLIE. Hold on. *(CHARLIE gently dials and lifts the phone to his ear.)* Hello this is Charlie. . . . Can you hear—

The mouthpiece falls into his lap. CHARLIE tosses it into the hay. ANGUS retrieves it.

ANGUS. Kinda rough on your tools.

CHARLIE. Okay, Angus, we gotta go.

ANGUS. Go where.

CHARLIE. Back to the home. I'll make this call from there.

ANGUS. I'm not going back anywheres.

CHARLIE. Unless you want to take a ride with me to Albany tonight . . .

ANGUS. Now why would a grown man want to go to New York state?

CHARLIE. Either you go back to the home, or come with me. You're not staying alone.

ANGUS. That's why I made two beds, Sam. Take your pick.

CHARLIE. Gramp, we are not sleeping in the barn.

ANGUS. Your relatives over in Scotland—

CHARLIE. Yeah you told me.

ANGUS. Your great great grandfather, Cyrus Stewart—

CHARLIE. Gramp, I do not—

ANGUS. No, you just listen. Here. *(HE pulls a pair of red needle-nose pliers from his pocket.)* Gimme that thing, I'll see what I can do. *(CHARLIE hands him the mouthpiece and receiver.)* Cyrus Stewart had a highland farm. Good, healthy herd, no reason to leave whatsoever, till one Christmas his son-in-law comes home with a present for the farm—first-calf Guernsey heifer. Now this is not only an *English* cow, but she's raised so close to France she can't even moo properly; comes out more like "mew." So she hasn't been there—hold on to that for me, will ya—she hasn't been there more than two three days, and it's a terrible cold night, whole family's sleepin' up in the loft, all bundled up, and Cyrus hears this "mew." Looks up, and there she is—the new Guernsey. *(HOPLEY appears. HE is dry, calm.)* So Cyrus starts explainin' about how the cows live downstairs, and then, in the dark behind her he notices all these puffs of steam—the whole damn herd is up there with her. And this new Guernsey, she's like the organizer, she says, "Excusez moi, but we are tired of providin' all the heat for you and your family."

CHARLIE. Stop.

ANGUS. Hold on. There's a moral.

CHARLIE. Angus, do you know what's going to happen when Marie gets wind of that fax? There is going to be a nuclear explosion and you are gonna end up in front of a judge, pleading sanity, okay? So from now on, you are going to practice being normal, okay? Saying normal things.

ANGUS. So I won't be declared impotent.

CHARLIE. Don't *do* that. Every time you do that, I'm going to stop you.

ANGUS. Do what?

CHARLIE. Pretend to not understand what's going on. You *know* what is going on.

ANGUS. So I'm not confused.

CHARLIE. No.

ANGUS. *(With a look to HOPLEY.)* Everything I think is happening, is happening.

CHARLIE. Yes.

ANGUS. . . . That's too bad.

CHARLIE. It's not too bad. It means you can trust what you see.

ANGUS. But what I see, there's too much, everything at once.

CHARLIE. That's just the way it is now. Things are happening, changes are coming faster and faster. It's like a free fall and you just have to—something makes sense, you grab it, something holds you back, get rid of it, whatever works. And some people just don't have the balls for that.

ANGUS. I had balls. *(HOPLEY turns and exits.)*

CHARLIE. I know. That's why I'm like this. That's why if I'm on a crowded sidewalk and I'm late or something—

this's happened two or three times—I picture myself running right on top of everyone. Right along their heads. Now I'm not particularly proud of that, but—

MARIE is at the top of the ladder. SHE carries a bag.

ANGUS. Hey look at this. Sam set up his little computer and phone thing and it's also a fax machine, isn't that something? Like the one out at the funeral home. Know what we're gonna do? We're gonna send them a fax, right Sam, we're gonna fax 'em a nice ripe cow turd . . . *(Pause.)*

CHARLIE. He's a little excited.

MARIE. So am I.

CHARLIE. Your lawyer called about the . . . change?

MARIE. Actually I was there when it came through. *(SHE pulls the fax from her bag.)* Unsigned. Here you go. *(SHE hands it to ANGUS, along with a pen. HE signs.)* I don't suppose you had a chance to look over the papers.

CHARLIE. I took a quick look, yeah . . . Marie, I do apologize for—

MARIE. Forget it. It's over.

CHARLIE. I'm just saying, if this thing goes to court, I don't want it to get personal.

MARIE. Well I sure as hell don't have any plans to go to court— You might as well go ahead and sign too. Everything official.

CHARLIE. You're certainly being a good sport.

MARIE. Why wouldn't I be? I've spent the last six years taking care of this man I don't even know how it happened, I just— I've got a big lap I guess. But now it's up to you.

CHARLIE. Well, Angus.

MARIE. Well, it's a little more complicated than that, because, let me see, I've got my list here. . . . Number one: retirement home. Russell and I have paid up through the end of the month, but of course after that, any residential costs—home health, whatever you want to do—would come back to you. Number two: prescriptions. Here you go, you'll want to make sure he gets the Medicaid discount on these. Three: I brought along some diapers for you. Angus can show you how to use those, and—

CHARLIE. Wait a minute.

MARIE. —that just leaves number 4. *(SHE produces a document.)* This is something you need to fill out and file down at the probate court before the closing tomorrow. And . . . that's that.

CHARLIE. "Acceptance of Guardianship"?

MARIE. It has to be transferred.

CHARLIE. I'm not— He is his own guardian now.

ANGUS. I have to do whatever I say?

CHARLIE. I didn't do this so I could take your place.

MARIE. You selfish little shit. This is exactly what I expected from you.

CHARLIE. He doesn't even want me around, Marie. He said so.

MARIE. It doesn't matter what he wants. Did you happen to look through the land trust papers?

CHARLIE. Quickly, yuh.

MARIE. Then maybe you didn't notice that the entire deal depends upon a particular contribution.

CHARLIE. The anonymous donor. I saw that.

MARIE. Did you also notice the *conditions* for that donation?

CHARLIE. I didn't *study* it.

MARIE. Why don't we study it together then? *(SHE finds the letter of intent.)* Here we go: "It shall be a condition precedent of this gift that the beneficiary, Angus Michael Stewart, shall designate a legal *guardian* with unlimited and irrevocable control over his legal, medical and business affairs." . . . What that means, Angus, is that either you find a new guardian by tomorrow morning or you can kiss your house, barn, the entire 420 acres goodbye. But I'm sure your management consultant friend here will think of something. *(SHE starts to exit.)* By the way. You try breaking into the house, I will have you arrested. Cindy pays Angus 675 dollars a month to keep the place to herself.

CHARLIE. Marie—

MARIE. *Don't even start* . . . Russell has been telling me for years that there is something in this family that insists on destroying itself and I have argued, I have . . . I was so stupid I thought maybe if we could just hang on to this place, then somehow the rest could work itself out.

ANGUS. *(As MARIE exits:)* Now you know better.

CHARLIE. Stay here.

ANGUS. Where you think you're going?

CHARLIE. To stop her.

ANGUS. I told ya, we're not going anywheres till we get this hay in.

CHARLIE. Listen, I don't have time right—

ANGUS. No, you listen. Hear that wind? When that rain hits, we're gonna have about 15 acres of mildew out there.

CHARLIE. Look. Don't do this right now.

ANGUS. The word is no, Sam. First we get the hay in, then—

CHARLIE. I don't have time! You stupid man. I have other people in my life! *(ANGUS pulls out his belt.)* I will be right back. *(CHARLIE climbs down.)*

ANGUS. Don't you walk out on me GOD DAMN YOU . . . You climb down that ladder you will never come back here again! *(ANGUS stops. To himself:)* Never.

HOPLEY steps out and pulls the pitchfork from the haystack. HE stabs the fork into one of the straw beds and pitches it onto the other. HE hands ANGUS the pitchfork. ANGUS tidies up, making a single bed out of the two. CROSSFADE to YOUNG ANGUS and MAE in the high loft. As before, the only light comes through the window.

MAE. It's still dark, probably an hour before dawn on the fourth day, when the rain finally stops. It will be another two days before the river starts to recede. In the window across the way, your mother still sits in her chair, your sister dozing in her lap. . . . It barely makes a sound when the land under the house gives way. *(LIGHT dims.)* There is a momentary pause. The window slowly sinks, makes a sudden turn . . . then it's gone. *(BLACKOUT.)*

END ACT 1

ACT II

ANGUS is splitting scrap wood and tossing it on a pile. MAE and YOUNG ANGUS look out from the high loft.

MAE. When the waters finally recede, the valley will be a carpet of stones, great boulders that a team of six can barely move. Down along the intervale, covering the crow-black soil, there will be a bed of sand, up to nine feet thick in some places. . . . But on the morning of the fourth day, we still look out on a world of water, stranded in this upside-down ark. Down below, the livestock shift their weight, ankle-deep in water.

ANGUS. You gonna make it easy on me, gimme those matches . . . or do I have to do this like a cave man? . . .

MAE. I haven't finished my story.

ANGUS. *(Tries to spark a flame with the ax and stone.)* I know how it ends.

MAE. Not my version, you don't. . . . It's been 16 hours since we saw Hopley Stewart swallowed, tossed up, and swept away by the raging waters. For all we know, Angus is the only Stewart left. Then he appears. Back from the dead . . .

HOPLEY climbs up from below, drenched and shivering. ANGUS watches, transfixed, as YOUNG ANGUS hurries down. The boy jumps up but HOPLEY turns away.

MAE. No hug, no tears. No words to explain or console.

Not even a pat on the shoulder. Just a reminder—whatever happens in the world, cows still need milking. *(HOPLEY gestures for YOUNG ANGUS to head down the ladder. HOPLEY waits for YOUNG ANGUS to disappear. He cradles his arm and lowers himself onto the bed of hay.)* You see, Angus? There's something you didn't know. He wasn't angry that you hadn't come to find him. Or disgusted or anything. He was in shock with a dislocated shoulder.

ANGUS. Grandpa? . . . Grandpa, you okay? Do you need something? Some water? . . . 'Course you don't need water, you're half-drowned. How 'bout some food? Are you hungry? We've got some— *(Picks up the McDonalds bag.)* Scottish food . . . *(HOPLEY turns away. ANGUS tosses the bag down the opening.)*

CHARLIE. *(From below.)* Hey, careful up there.

ANGUS. I told you to never come back here again. *(Slams the trap door shut and bolts it. CHARLIE pounds from below.)*

ANGUS. Go away. *(A look from HOPLEY.)* What? . . . Grandpa, I tried every damn thing I know. You saw for yourself, he doesn't want to work, doesn't want to be here. He doesn't want to know what I know. Look, I'm not complaining, but when you were old, I did it all. Seventeen years old and I ran this place by myself. Now there's no one.

MAE. *(To AUDIENCE.)* That's what he's like when he's not complaining.

ANGUS. I'm just saying, a boy isn't like a farm-hand you can just hire.

MAE. Yeah, it's hard to get good sons these days.

ANGUS. Stay out of this, you.

MAE. You're not stupid, Angus, what's wrong with you? You got a boy pounding on the door wants to help you and you say you have no help.

ANGUS. He had his chance! . . . He doesn't care. How could he? *(Climbing to the high loft.)* He looks out there, he doesn't see the fields like they were. Or the intervale, my dad down there with the oxen, one beer upstream, one beer down, plowin' his way back and forth between sips. He can't see the house that used to be right there, or the window. . . . No one could see all that, and leave.

MAE. Then you have to show him.

ANGUS. Is that what you want, Grandpa? One more try?

CHARLIE. *(From below.)* Angus, open the goddam door or I will break it . . . *(MAE looks at ANGUS, who nods. She unbolts the door and exits.)* ANGUS! *(The trap door blasts open. CHARLIE climbs up.)* All right, where— *(HE spots ANGUS in the high loft.)* Jesus Christ. What are you doing up there?

ANGUS. I'm with a woman, Sam, and I'll ask you to keep your voice down.

CHARLIE. Look, I'm coming up. *Don't* move.

ANGUS. Have to move a little, Sam. Otherwise they lose interest. . . . Actually, you better stay down. Three of us up here, the thing's liable to drop.

CHARLIE. I would like to talk to you. About tonight.

ANGUS. I know what you mean. Whenever I'm watching dusk, I'm thinking, this beats the hell out of dawn. Animals feel it too, they like a slow change in the air. Next morning though, just before light, I'm putting on my boots goin', *dawn,* ya know. Beats the hell out of dusk.

CHARLIE. I have a proposal for you.

ANGUS. Tell ya what: you come up here, take a good long look at this view . . . whatever you want, I'll say yes.

CHARLIE. Please come down.

ANGUS. Jesus. This better be good. *(Grabs a rope and prepares to swing down.)* Look out.

CHARLIE. Angus!

ANGUS. You're no fun. *(Climbs down. Points to a new rip in Charlie's shirt.)* Jeez, look at you. You're comin' apart.

CHARLIE. Can we sit? *(ANGUS sits.)* Angus, you know there's a lot going on right now, lot up in the air. You've got a closing scheduled tomorrow, tied up with the whole guardianship thing, right? . . . Angus?

ANGUS. I'm waitin' for the proposal part.

CHARLIE. I just want to make sure we're clear. Because this is big stuff. We don't want to rush into. So what I propose is we postpone the closing so I can go off, take care of business, take care of . . . things. That means right now, tonight, I take you back to the home, temporarily, and then first thing Saturday morning I pick you up, we go sit down over breakfast—not thinking about all this other stuff—we start looking five, ten years down the road, where do you want to be, because that's what I do. Now before you say anything—

ANGUS. Okay.

CHARLIE. What?

ANGUS. *(Starting down the ladder.)* Thought we were leaving.

CHARLIE. So you understand and all. You agree?

ANGUS. Sam, I'm old, I'm not stupid. . . . Careful, there's a loose rung here.

CHARLIE. Hold on, I'll grab my stuff. . . . I think this is best. Ya know? And I'll be back Saturday. . . . You know what? I'll bring Nick. It's perfect, I think he'd— I mean the last time he was here he was in diapers. 'Member? *(ANGUS shakes his head.)* Yeah, we've got a picture of you holding him like this. Like a little hand puppet. The two of you, chattin' away.

ANGUS. This 'd be Saturday?

CHARLIE. That's what I was thinking. If I can work it out with Karen. Nick and I can stay in a hotel or something. Or maybe we'll just camp up here, that might be good.

ANGUS. Sure. You can bring him to the auction.

CHARLIE. What?

ANGUS. Or maybe not. Some kids don't enjoy an auction. I never much did.

CHARLIE. You're talking about the farm. This farm.

ANGUS. Yeah.

CHARLIE. This Saturday.

ANGUS. Yeah, see the bank likes a nice weekend auction.

More people, out-of-staters, whatever. I s'ppose that's why Marie scheduled the closing for tomorrow. Try to keep the auctioneer away.

CHARLIE. You knew this all along.

ANGUS. Well it's not like they foreclose without tellin' ya, Sam. They send a registered letter.

CHARLIE. Why didn't you say something?

ANGUS. I just did.

CHARLIE. I mean before, when I was going on about postponing and long-term planning and— Do you understand what's about to happen? Do you care?

ANGUS. I was trying to be agreeable.

CHARLIE. Jesus Christ. *(Starts for the ladder.)*

ANGUS. Don't forget your little machine over there.

CHARLIE. I'm not leaving, Angus. I can't just go, can I? After what you just said. . . . You don't make this easy. *(Starts down the ladder. The rung gives way, and he drops. HE ends up straddling the rung below, in acute pain.)*

ANGUS. That's that bad rung I mentioned. . . . How many kids you say you've got? . . . Boy, right? One boy? Well that's all it takes to carry on. We were down to one bull there, right after the flood. Didn't take more'n a couple years before the herd was full again. 'Course your males are pretty much expendable long as you got one . . . even then, only takes one good testicle.

CHARLIE. SHUT UP! . . . I am your last chance old man. Now you can smirk and mock me all you want. I'm an easy target, okay? I don't build things with my hands, I didn't suffer here my whole life. But I work like a goddam mule. . . . I'm a Stewart too, Angus. I was here, 'til I was 8. I jumped out of that loft, I itched. I threw bales. And I would like my son to have this too, okay? . . . Now I am willing to help, but if you're just going to waste my time with these stupid—

ANGUS. Sam, I wasn't wasting—

CHARLIE. My name is not Sam. My name is Charlie.

ANGUS. Whatever, I—

CHARLIE. No. Charlie. . . . Now look at me, and say my name.

ANGUS. Charlie.

CHARLIE. Good. . . . Thank you. . . . Now I am going to make some arrangements. Again. I am going to cancel some very important things, do you understand? And while I do, you are not going to climb any ladders, or chop down any buildings, you are going to sit. There. Until I get back. *(Exits.)*

ANGUS. *(To HOPLEY.)* Jeezum. Wonder what got into Sam . . .

MAE appears.

MAE. Shame on you. Making fun of him like that.

ANGUS. That's what we do. Man's in pain, you make a joke so he don't feel stupid.

MAE. How many times you think he's going to come back, old man? I thought you were going to try.

During the following, YOUNG ANGUS climbs up from below, holding a bottle of milk. HE offers it to HOPLEY, who lies shivering in the bed of hay.

ANGUS. I am. I just don't . . . How do you make sense of a person like that. Business man. How does he know he's a businessman? I mean a farmer doesn't choose what he is, he's just born on a farm. How do you decide what you are? I don't understand.

MAE. Then ask him. . . . Then try to listen. . . . *(HOPLEY refuses the milk and gestures for YOUNG ANGUS to drink it.)* Should I tell them why you had sores and rashes all the time until you were twelve? . . . Come on, Angus, you have to laugh. Imagine that, a farm boy who's allergic to milk.

YOUNG ANGUS drinks. MAE exits. CHARLIE climbs up carrying a paper bag and a lantern. ANGUS reaches for the bag.

CHARLIE. *(Pulling it away.)* First work, then eat. . . . You have a decision to make. . . . Option A. You sign this "VOLUNTARY GUARDIANSHIP" form, we drive over to Marie's, apologize up and down till she signs it. Tomorrow morning, 10:00, she closes on the land trust deal. End of story.

ANGUS. Two conditions: No and never.

CHARLIE. Wait a minute, before you dismiss it—

ANGUS. No. Marie will not change her mind, get that out of

your head, the woman is French Indian, and never, ever, ever, will I sell the *right* to use my property, so get that out of your head too.

CHARLIE. That's not what—

ANGUS. "Keep the leg, Mr. Stewart, it's all yours. You just can't walk on it."

CHARLIE. It's only for devel—

ANGUS. No and never. Next.

CHARLIE. Okay. Option B. Do nothing. Auction on Saturday, then you go . . . wherever you want.

ANGUS. . . . This is what you get paid to do?

CHARLIE. We haven't got to "C" yet.

ANGUS. Oh "C." I'm glad there's C.

CHARLIE. Okay look, maybe this whole land trust deal is an over-reaction. I total up your back tax liability, arrearage with the bank—you've got this second mortgage—but even with penalties, you're only talking . . . 30, 32 thousand.

ANGUS. Spencer owes me 20 though . . . dollars.

CHARLIE. I'm just saying if we can wipe out this short-term debt, then all we have to do is generate some regular income. We're not talking about a fortune.

ANGUS. What are we talking about?

CHARLIE. You. Here. Full-time. Running the show.

ANGUS. Me.

CHARLIE. That's right. You become the manager slash owner.

ANGUS. Manager slash owner. . . . Of what?

CHARLIE. The new enterprise, whatever form it takes. Driving range, RV campground, maybe we renovate the barn for storage, mix and match, keep it simple, no big development. The place stays pretty much as it is. The big change, Gramp, is that you are your own boss again. *(CHARLIE puts the bag down in front of ANGUS.)* Go ahead. *(ANGUS looks in.)* Rice cakes, gatorade, couple granny smiths. *(ANGUS pulls out something.)* That's a power bar. It's good.

ANGUS. *(Tosses it back in the bag, unimpressed.)* Cindy food. *(HOPLEY whispers to ANGUS.)*

CHARLIE. Hey I risked my life for that stuff. I get halfway in the kitchen window and this vicious mongrel comes—

ANGUS. What about livestock?

CHARLIE. What?

ANGUS. This option C, what if we want to have animals?

CHARLIE. Then you have animals. You want a couple chickens or a goat. Hey, it's your farm.

ANGUS. What about you?

CHARLIE. I'd be like a partner. Silent partner.

ANGUS. How silent?

CHARLIE. That's something we'd work out. Right now what we need to focus on is the short-term picture.

ANGUS. You mean money.

CHARLIE. Partly, yes.

ANGUS. Thought that's what silent partners were for.

CHARLIE. Well, unfortunately my money is tied up at the moment, but that doesn't mean—

ANGUS. I figured.

CHARLIE. Gramp, I am swimming in legal shit right now. If I could, I would write you a check in a minute, you *know* that. . . . I do have an idea though . . .

ANGUS. I'm listening.

CHARLIE. Down along the intervale, that whole bank, where we used to swim, that's sand, right? Clean white sand.

ANGUS. Dig down far enough, used to be two feet of topsoil.

CHARLIE. Then let's put it back. The way it was, let's haul that sand out of there, I've got clients who would buy in.

ANGUS. Sell the sand? *(A look passes between ANGUS and HOPLEY.)* No.

CHARLIE. What do you mean "no". You can't just— Look, we sell the sand, not the land.

ANGUS. He put that sand there for a reason, Sam.

CHARLIE. What, like it's some curse you're supposed to just live with?

ANGUS. No.

CHARLIE. Then what?

ANGUS. I'd just rather not go wakin' people up might be restin' under there.

CHARLIE. Well yeah, I can see why that's, I mean, okay . . . but Gramp, do *you* see, how it's the same thing? You want something, but you keep making it impossible. At some point you either let all this past stuff suffocate you, or— change is not always bad. *(HOPLEY whispers to ANGUS.)*

ANGUS. What about sheep?

CHARLIE. We're not talking about that. *(HOPLEY gestures for ANGUS to offer CHARLIE some chew.)* Gramp, we're not dickering here.

ANGUS. Go ahead. Won't hurt ya.

CHARLIE. I'm spaced enough already.

ANGUS. Calm ya right down.

CHARLIE. All right, but we're talking about one thing at a time.

ANGUS. Seems kind of inefficient but, okay. *(Takes a pinch.)* Right down in here.

CHARLIE. I know, I know. I played Babe Ruth League. *(HOPLEY confers with ANGUS, who turns to CHARLIE.)*

ANGUS. We need two rams and 40 ewes for breeding right away. Plus feed. Fencing.

CHARLIE. Wait a minute, first—

ANGUS. Rest of the sand money goes to retire the debt. That's the deal. Sand for sheep. . . . Or are we just talking?

CHARLIE. No, I'm just not clear on, I mean what's the market we're hitting here? Vermont *sheep?* I don't know, is that—

ANGUS. Used to be six sheep to every person in this state.

CHARLIE. Okay, so it's historical, that's . . . maybe some kind of specialty cheese, Vermont organic, that sort of thing . . .

ANGUS. Dairy sheep?

CHARLIE. Sure. We sell it locally, however much you produce. All the little Mom and Pop stores. Tourists come in, "Mmmm. This looks interesting." They tell their friends. Maybe we find some specialty shop in the city . . . *(HOPLEY mimes milking tiny sheep udders. ANGUS laughs.)* Look, this was your idea.

ANGUS. No. Sorry, it's just, when you think about it . . . *(ANGUS and HOPLEY mime it together. They crack up.)*

CHARLIE. Fine. Forget it. . . . I'm trying to meet you halfway, but go ahead.

ANGUS. These things take time, Sam.

CHARLIE. I can't help it. As a potential partner, you start acting this way, it worries me.

ANGUS. Hey, I worry myself. Marie must have told you I have these spells.

CHARLIE. Is that what the estrogen is for?

ANGUS. No, that's so I won't be such a horny bugger, staring at Cindy all day. No, the spells, what do they call 'em—"lucid intervals."

CHARLIE. Lucid.

ANGUS. Yeah. That's when you're thinking clearly.

CHARLIE. I know. . . . That's a problem?

ANGUS. Well, yeah. Because, for me anyway, the more lucid I get, the less sense everything makes. It's like manure. Used to be fertilizer, right? Now you gotta pay some fella to come take it away. Then you gotta pay another fella to bring your fertilizer. That's called progress. . . . You got people working two, three hours away from home, kids don't even know what they do for work. That's freedom. Then you got people actually *buying* green apples. . . . So everyone knows I have these lucid intervals, we just can't seem to agree on when they are. . . . What do you think? Am I making sense right now?

CHARLIE. Yes.

ANGUS. So, when don't I make sense?

CHARLIE. Well you— you want me to just tell you?

ANGUS. If we're gonna be working together . . .

CHARLIE. Well . . . you do talk to yourself.

ANGUS. Now that's not true.

CHARLIE. Okay, well . . .

ANGUS. No, I may talk to people who are not entirely there, but I have never talked to myself. No point to it.

CHARLIE. Right.

ANGUS. So, do I pass?

CHARLIE. It's not that.

ANGUS. Why not? We're making a deal. You want to know what you're getting into. So do I.

CHARLIE. Go ahead then. Ask away.

ANGUS. Well, you're a business man, you work in a city, right?

CHARLIE. Yeah.

ANGUS. So you, have jobs and you do them all day and then um . . . how do you know when you're done?

CHARLIE. I just decide.

ANGUS. But how? Do you finish everything and then start again or . . .

CHARLIE. Sometimes. I'm not sure I understand.

ANGUS. Me neither. . . . Tell me about Option D.

CHARLIE. We only got to C.

ANGUS. I know. Option D is the one where you come home, Sam. And you work with me and when you're done everyday, you'll know why.

CHARLIE. See, that's what I like about Option C, Gramp, because we'd be business partners.

ANGUS. Business?

CHARLIE. Yeah.

ANGUS. So what's in it for you?

CHARLIE. Nothing.

ANGUS. Then it ain't business.

CHARLIE. Things stay the way they are. That matters to me. It matters that you are where you should be.

ANGUS. And where should *you* be? California?

CHARLIE. I'm in New York. . . . Gramp, I'm a phone call away.

ANGUS. *(Pointing to the broken parts.)* That phone?

CHARLIE. Gramp look. Right now, I'm all over the place, that's how I make my living, I hustle. The people I see, my friends, they're the people I work with. I don't have friends outside work. So I'm saying, why not work together, then I would *have* to be around more?

ANGUS. Animals like to eat every day, ya know. There's chores every day.

CHARLIE. Then we'll *get* somebody. Maybe this, what's his name, Cindy's boyfriend. If we decide that's—

ANGUS. You want this farm, but you don't want to do anything to earn it.

CHARLIE. That's not true.

ANGUS. You want to use the truck, you want to have your girlfriends up here.

CHARLIE. What are you talking about?

ANGUS. *(Overlapping.)* But when there's work to do, Sam, you've always got a reason to be somewhere else.

CHARLIE. I'm not Sam.

ANGUS. Right. You're no son of mine. Now get out of here. . . . I said get.

CHARLIE. No.

ANGUS. GET OUT!

CHARLIE. I'm staying.

ANGUS. *(Picks up the pitchfork.)* I may not be able to make you stay, but I can sure as hell make you go. *(HE lunges at CHARLIE, who sidesteps.)* Get out boy. I'm giving you your excuse, now get. *(CHARLIE stands his ground.)* Here. *(ANGUS drives the pitchfork through the laptop.)* Take your toys with ya. *(HE pitches it down the opening. We hear the CRASH.) (Pause.)*

CHARLIE. I'm not leaving, Angus.

ANGUS. Then you're next.

CHARLIE. Just like Dad? Just like Russell? You drive us all away, don't you? One by one, we all fail you. We all turn out be lazy, or foolish, or disloyal. No one meets your standards, why is that?

ANGUS. Because you believe in nothing. Stand for nothing. You say you don't want the farm, then what the hell do you want? . . . You stand there, willing to take a pitchfork in the belly and you don't even know why. . . . Do you!

CHARLIE. . . . No.

ANGUS hurls the pitchfork into the hay. CHARLIE turns, and climbs into the high loft. MAE appears.

MAE. He may stand for nothing, old man, but. at least he stands.

ANGUS. It's all just business to him. He doesn't care what happens to this place. You notice how he jumped at Option D.

During the following, HOPLEY rises, picks up the pitchfork and with his good arm pitches some hay down the opening.

MAE. Some people, you threaten them with a pitchfork, or an ax, or you kick them in the face, next thing they don't want to be around you.

ANGUS. You think it's funny?

MAE. Yes I think it's funny, how you two are so close to agreeing but you're too stupid to see it.

ANGUS. So now I *am* stupid.

HOPLEY grabs his shoulder, seized with pain. MAE starts toward him but he shakes his head.

MAE. *(To AUDIENCE.)* Watch. This explains a lot about the Stewart men. *(HOPLEY slips his injured arm around a post. He yanks, trying to pop his shoulder back into socket.)* Oops. One more time. *(HOPLEY prepares for another try.)* You know what? I'd rather be him right now than him. *(Gesturing to CHARLIE in the high loft.)* Trying to negotiate with you.

ANGUS. I've tried everything I know.

MAE. You should probably quit then. . . . I'm serious. Quit trying. We've seen what happens when you try . . .

ANGUS. So I should . . .

MAE. Try not to try.

ANGUS. That makes no sense.

MAE. You've tried everything you know. Try something you don't . . .

ANGUS. Try not to try. *(She nods.)* That makes no sense.

HOPLEY blacks out and collapses behind the haystack.

MAE. Self-reliance.

MAE exits. ANGUS looks up at CHARLIE, begins to speak, then stops. He sits, confused. A dog barks.

ANGUS. Go get 'em, Pete. *(Dog barks again.)* Hear that? That's Pete. Hardest workin' cow dog ever. When my Dad first got sick, he told me all I had to do was step outside and shout, "Go get 'em, Pete," and the cows would come in. And it worked. They would come just about stampeding across the road to get in the barn. They knew better than to mess with Pete.

CHARLIE. Angus, that can't be Pete. He would be dead.

ANGUS. 'Course he's dead, but we didn't tell the cows that. Pete was in the ground maybe two years I could still step out and holler, "Go get 'em, Pete." Cows 'd come running. *(Dog barks.)* You don't hear that?

CHARLIE. Yeah. I do.

ANGUS. Good. I'm not hearing things then . . . or at least we both are. . . . What are you lookin' at up there?

CHARLIE. Nothing, I'm just . . .

ANGUS. Should be chargin' ya for that view. Moonlight in Vermont, you know what that goes for?

CHARLIE. . . . Hard to believe there was a house right there. How big was it?

ANGUS. Big. Too big.

CHARLIE. Too big?

ANGUS. Easy target. That's the big joke. Cyrus Stewart builds this great big house, everyone says, oh Cyrus, come winter you're gonna wish you connected right up to the barn so you won't have to step outside. Cyrus says no sir, I'd rather put up with the cold than give the Lord a chance to clean us out with one bolt of lightning. . . . So He sends a river instead.

CHARLIE. And your whole family was in there?

ANGUS. No, my dad was already gone from typhus, or typhoid, I forget which. Whichever one kills ya. . . . I notice you're still here, that's good. I'm uh . . .

CHARLIE. We'll see how good it is. I don't do something quick, I'm going down in history as the asshole who lost this place.

ANGUS. Have to fight me for that title. *(Dog barks.)*
CHARLIE. Go get 'em, Pete.

An overhead light blinks on. SPENCER enters from below. HE wears a softball uniform. CHARLIE watches from the high loft.

SPENCER. What t' hell? She just leave you up here? *(HE inspects the food next to ANGUS. He takes an apple.)* Looks like she got you all moved in. Musta pissed her off pretty good. . . . I don't know, Angus, you might want to think about apologizin'. Long about January it's gonna be pretty chilly up here . . . *(SPENCER suddenly yanks out the high loft ladder, stranding CHARLIE.)* All right mister you're not going anywhere 'til you tell me who you are and what you're doing up here.
CHARLIE. Wait, you don't under—
SPENCER. Get back from the edge. You try jumpin', I'll break your leg 'fore you hit the ground.
CHARLIE. I'm Charlie.
SPENCER. . . . Charlie who?
CHARLIE. Charlie Stewart, I'm his grandson.
SPENCER. You're the Pathfinder?
CHARLIE. Yes. You must be—
SPENCER. What're you doin' up there?
CHARLIE. I was just looking out . . . Can you . . . ? *(Gesturing to return the ladder.)*
SPENCER. Looking out at what?
CHARLIE. The view.

SPENCER. It's dark out.

CHARLIE. But there was no light in here . . . and with the moon—

SPENCER. Reason I come up is I noticed a light flickering. Thought there might be some juvenile delinquents up here, startin' a fire.

ANGUS. Just us.

SPENCER. He speaks. *(SPENCER replaces the ladder.)*

CHARLIE. So you must be Cindy's boyfriend, right?

SPENCER. We're pretty much engaged. *(Shaking hands.)* Spencer Eddy.

CHARLIE. Charlie Stewart, I'm actually glad you're here. We were just talking about you.

SPENCER. *(To ANGUS.)* Got ya talkin' again, did he? Y' old bastard.

CHARLIE. We've been kicking around ideas for how to hang on to this place.

SPENCER. Cindy's mom has that all worked out.

CHARLIE. We were thinking of other ideas though, running the place more like a business. That's when your name came up.

SPENCER. Yeah?

CHARLIE. I don't know what you've got going already but, we would probably be looking for someone, part-time ya know.

SPENCER. Part-time what?

CHARLIE. Well, for example, if there were animals, there'd be chores.

SPENCER. You mean shovelin' shit.

CHARLIE. Not necessarily. There's room for a lot more.

SPENCER. More shit?

CHARLIE. More money . . . for more responsibility. You handle the day to day stuff, that's one thing. You do some managing, that's more. Maybe you oversee scheduling the daycare, or maybe you do some of it yourself, all these things have a value. . . . Now of course I don't know what your present situation is in terms of work.

SPENCER. Got plenty . . . always looking for something though, if it pays.

CHARLIE. So you might be interested?

SPENCER. I try to never turn down a job I haven't been offered.

CHARLIE. This would be more of a partnership. You, Angus and me.

SPENCER. You're the investor.

CHARLIE. More of a consultant.

SPENCER. So where's the money come from?

CHARLIE. *(With a wink to ANGUS.)* Well, we've still got to make a little progress in that direction but . . . I think we've got that covered.

SPENCER. You wanna know what would make some money around here and this is something I've talked to Cindy about, though it's only seasonal and it's a shitload of work, but I've been thinking, there's all that beautiful topsoil down in the intervale, we could have one hell of a garden and with Cindy it would all have to be organic, which means people would pay more, but instead of takin' produce into the natural food store, where I'm sick of losing—you know with my syrup, there goes 35 percent right off the top—so I say we set Angus right up there next to the road . . . *(To ANGUS.)* In your own little farm stand and you can sit there with your vegetables, say nothing, collect money all day. Just you and Boo.

CHARLIE. That's something you'd be willing to work on?

SPENCER. Shit yes. Well I shouldn't say that with a couple beers in me but, Christ if you got some money to put into this place I say that's the way to go.

ANGUS. You owe me twenty dollars.

SPENCER. Now he's talkin'.

CHARLIE. This sounds—I mean how soon could we do this?

SPENCER. See that's the thing. If we knew *now,* we could fertilize, get some winter rye planted, that place 'd be primed and ready first thing in the spring. We can get this old fella down there scarin' crows away.

CHARLIE. What about the sand?

SPENCER. What sand?

CHARLIE. Covering the topsoil.

SPENCER. Christ they trucked that out of there six seven years ago. It's part of the bypass now. Guess you haven't been down there for a while.

CHARLIE. No.

SPENCER. We can take a walk down there tomorrow. Wait 'til you get a look at that topsoil, man, it is black. You plant a rock down there, it'd probably grow.

CHARLIE. Yeah.

SPENCER. You wanna come up for a beer? Cindy's got her class tonight.

CHARLIE. No, that's okay thanks. We're just gonna . . . catch up a little.

SPENCER. Yeah, I gotta eat . . . *(Exiting.)* I guess probably Marie doesn't know you're here, right? I mean I won't tell her.

CHARLIE. That's probably . . . thanks.

SPENCER. Don't want to tangle with her. Come find me tomorrow.

CHARLIE. Yeah. *(SPENCER exits.)*

ANGUS. Twenty dollars! . . . And turn that goddam light out! *(Turning away from CHARLIE.)* You'd think he worked for the power company, way he wastes electric.

Pause. OVERHEAD LIGHT goes out.

CHARLIE. You're good, Angus.

ANGUS. Me?

CHARLIE. Oh yeah, you should be proud. The bit about not wanting to sell, not wanting to disturb the dead . . . very touching.

ANGUS. What is it we're fighting about?

CHARLIE. Just *don't,* okay? You knew, you lied. Just admit it.

ANGUS. You get to be my age, Sam, you can only get at a certain amount of what you know on any given day.

CHARLIE. No. That is too easy. One minute you make perfect sense, we seem to be getting somewhere, next thing you're back to—

ANGUS. I'm old, damn it.

CHARLIE. No, you are spiteful. You are crawling with hate. And you will not be happy until everyone of us is just as miserable as you.

ANGUS. The son is supposed to take of the father. He cares for the father.

CHARLIE. My father did not *want* to leave you. . . . He wanted to stay. He told me what happened.

ANGUS. I offer you this farm and you spit in my face.

CHARLIE. That's not true. He made you a proposition. He said, "I'll stay and take over, but we *have to modernize.*"

ANGUS. You blackmail your own father.

CHARLIE. It was an offer. A deal. We clear out the basement, put in a concrete floor and move the cows down.

ANGUS. Spendin' money we don't have.

CHARLIE. The floor was rotting anyway, something had to be done.

A THUNDEROUS CRASH from below shakes the building.

ANGUS. Jesus. The floor!

CHARLIE. What?

ANGUS. Under Roosevelt! The floor gave way. *(We hear the choked bellowing of the bull.)* He's hanging! He's chained to the post, Sam. Hanging! Get the ax.

CHARLIE. Where?

ANGUS. The ice ax! *(CHARLIE looks for the ax.)*

VOICE OF SAM. *(From below.)* I can't chop the chain.

ANGUS. Chop below it. Chop the post. *(From below, the chopping of wood.)* Jesus, Sam, hurry. *(Chopping intensifies.)*

VOICE OF SAM. It's dull!

ANGUS. Put some muscle into it!

CHARLIE. What's happening?

ANGUS. He's strangling, for Christ's sake. Hurry, Sam!

VOICE OF SAM. It's too dull!

ANGUS. Then try the chain! See if you can break the chain. *(SOUND of the AX AGAINST STEEL.)* Hurry for Christ's sake . . . *(Chopping intensifies, then stops.)* What happened? Why d'ya stop? . . .

VOICE OF SAM. I'm gonna lift him.

ANGUS. You can't lift him!

VOICE OF SAM. I have to!

ANGUS. YOU CAN'T LIFT—

VOICE OF SAM. I HAVE TO! *(Bellowing and shouts from below build . . . then fade to silence. ANGUS slowly walks away.)*

ANGUS. This is where you leave, Sam. Go ahead. I don't blame you . . .

CHARLIE. Gramp, what just happened? Are you—

ANGUS. That's the last of 'em down there. A line starts all the way back in Scotland, right across the ocean 'til it ends, right here, with me.

CHARLIE. And me.

ANGUS. . . . Just go. *(ANGUS picks up the diaper bag and steps behind the haystack, out of sight.)* Not that complicated, farming. Keep your ax sharp, your floors solid. . . . You keep your boys to home.

CHARLIE. Gramp, he didn't leave you, he left the farm.

ANGUS. Don't come back here.

CHARLIE. He would have stayed, but the place was too small. It couldn't support two families.

ANGUS. You don't leave what you care for.

CHARLIE. But he did. I've seen, I visited Dad last year out West, he was drinking, he was talking about the farm. Listen to me, you could see that inside—

ANGUS. No!

CHARLIE. If he could make that choice again— *(Stares down on ANGUS, dumbstruck.)*

ANGUS. What's a matter? . . . Never seen a man without his testicles? *(CHARLIE staggers away.)* Makes it easier to clean around. See? Nothing in the way. . . . Don't worry, Sam, I'm not gonna ask ya to help.

MAE appears.

MAE. Used to be when a cow dropped dead in the barn, Hopley would hitch up the team and drag her out with a long rope. Big procedure, working around corners, through doorways, out across the gravel. I could always tell because the hide was smooth on one side. *(HOPLEY emerges from behind the haystack, barely able to stand. HE crosses to the bed of hay and falls into it.)* I used to wonder, what if one of the *oxen* dies? How do you move an animal twice the size of a cow with half the team? And that's his old partner on the floor. I suppose when the *last* of the team dies, you just hope he drops—

ANGUS. *(Stepping out into view.)* Get out of here, y'old. crow, I ain't droppin' yet.

MAE. Angus, this story is going to finish, whether you're ready or not.

ANGUS. Then it doesn't matter if I'm ready. *(Goes to the milk can and washes his hands.)* You just don't like the idea I might die before this place gets turned over to your daughter and all the other vultures.

MAE. Is that so bad, to care about the living? How can you give up so easy?

ANGUS. I tried everything. Then I tried nothing. What's left?

MAE. Maybe you let someone else try.

ANGUS. You?

MAE. I was thinking someone higher up.

ANGUS. Marie?

MAE. At this point, old man, anybody offers you a hand, you better say yes. *(Covers HOPLEY with her shawl.)* You better say, "Yes, thank you."

HOPLEY tosses off the shawl. MAE picks it up and exits.

CHARLIE. Gramp, nobody told me you had an operation.

ANGUS. Me neither. I swear. Just woke up one morning, went to scratch myself . . . and missed. Have to talk to Proxmire about that, messed up my whole plumbing system.

CHARLIE. Was it cancer?

ANGUS. I hate to think he'd do that for a cold.

CHARLIE. . . . Did they get it all?

ANGUS. You tell me. You got a better view than I can, he leave me anything?

CHARLIE. Stop.

ANGUS. Stop what?

CHARLIE. Joking about it.

ANGUS. . . . It helps. *(Pause.)*

CHARLIE. How long?

ANGUS. How long, he says. You're just like that goddam Proxmire, wants to tell me how long. How ever long *He* wants . . . Kinda raises hell with your long-term plans, huh?

CHARLIE. Forget about that, I just— Why didn't you tell me?

ANGUS. Tell ya the truth, Sam, I'm not too sure these days what's happened and what's gonna happen. But I'm glad you're here, or that you will be. *(CHARLIE goes to the folders.)* What 're you lookin for now? . . . You love those papers, don't ya? *(CHARLIE holds up an official form.)*

CHARLIE. You know what this is?

ANGUS. That's that guardian form again. I told ya I'm not going back to Marie with this.

CHARLIE. That's not what I had in mind. . . . I was thinking about Option D, how this could be part of it.

ANGUS. You.

CHARLIE. Why not?

ANGUS. You're gonna be my mother?

CHARLIE. No, I'm gonna be your guardian. I'm gonna sign here, and you're gonna sign there.

ANGUS. Then what? You gonna move up here?

CHARLIE. If I have to. Everything's sort of, all over the map now anyway. I can be based wherever. . . . Get Nick up here, I think he'd, you know? He might like having a few sheep.

ANGUS. Wait a minute. Who's Nick?

CHARLIE. That's my boy.

ANGUS. So if we both sign that thing . . . there'd be a little Stewart boy running around here? Swinging from the rafters. Jumpin' in the hay?

CHARLIE. That's right. But Gramp, that means we have to hang on to this place. That means you and I have a closing tomorrow.

ANGUS. Fine.

CHARLIE. We'd be keeping the farm and selling the development rights. You understand that, right?

ANGUS. Yup.

CHARLIE. And I would be watching out for ya, legally. Okay?

ANGUS. Yes . . . thanks.

CHARLIE. *(Signing.)* Well, you're welcome. *(Hands it to ANGUS.)* After the closing, we'll go out and have a big fat breakfast.

ANGUS. "Charles A. Stewart."

CHARLIE. Guess what the "A" is for.

ANGUS. You're Charlie?

CHARLIE. That's right.

ANGUS. Where's Sam?

CHARLIE. He's in California. *(ANGUS drops the form.)* Gramp, it's okay. I can do this. I can take care of you.

ANGUS. You're not my son.

CHARLIE. That doesn't mean I— Gramp, don't do this.

ANGUS. If he cared he would be here.

CHARLIE. This has nothing to do with how Dad feels about you. He's lives 3000 miles away.

ANGUS. If he cared—

CHARLIE. Gramp, listen. There are a lot of people, not just in the past and not just Stewarts who want to protect this place. There are people who have never even seen this property, willing to pay to keep it from being developed, all right? . . . Are you really so committed to honoring the dead that you're going to ignore all these people, all this help? *(Holds out a pen and the form.)* You're going to watch this place be swept away . . . again? *(ANGUS takes them.)*

ANGUS. Wish I didn't have to say yes. *(Places them in the hay and walks away. CHARLIE collapses into the hay.)*

MAE appears.

MAE. All day and night I listen for the last breath of Hopley Stewart. I wonder how long a man can cool before the fire in him is finally out. When I see that you're asleep, I go to Hopley and whisper, "Don't worry about Angus. He'll come live with us." "Am I dying," he asks, and I tell him, "Yes. You're going cold." *(SHE offers the shawl.)* "Better warm me then," he says. *(MAE covers him with the shawl.)*

ANGUS. You saved my grandfather?

MAE. He saved himself, Angus. By saying yes.

ANGUS looks at CHARLIE, who's asleep. ANGUS looks to the high loft: NICK, a boy in contemporary clothes, sits playing on Charlie's laptop computer.

ANGUS. Jesus, who's that?

MAE. Shhh. Who do you think?

ANGUS. Nick? Is that— *(Calling up.)* Nick! Get down here. Come say hi to your old . . . whatever I am. . . . He can't hear me.

MAE. We can.

ANGUS. What the hell is he doing up there? *(HOPLEY, MAE and ANGUS stare up at NICK, who is lost in his computer game.)*

MAE. . . . We'll never know.

MAE and HOPLEY exit, taking the lantern. ANGUS watches NICK in the moonlight. Finally, ANGUS settles in next to CHARLIE. Uncomfortable, ANGUS reaches under himself and pulls out the form and pen. A dog barks. NICK stands, looks out.

NICK. Go get 'em, Pete.

SOFT RAIN. ANGUS looks down at the form. Above him, NICK grabs a rope and tests if it will hold him.

BIRD SONG. MORNING LIGHT shines in. SPENCER shoots up the ladder. CHARLIE stirs.

SPENCER. She's comin'.

CHARLIE. What?

SPENCER. She's comin' and you're late.

CHARLIE. For what?

SPENCER. Closing. *(To ANGUS.)* Come on. Wake up, y'old—

CHARLIE. Shh. Wait. . . . We're not going.

SPENCER. You're not going?

CHARLIE. He won't sign the guardianship form.

SPENCER. So.

CHARLIE. So the deal's off. It's a condition of the agreement.

SPENCER. Agh, we just get Sam to fix it. Come on.

CHARLIE. Sam knows the anonymous donor?

SPENCER. Well yeah. It's him.

CHARLIE. Dad is— How do you know?

SPENCER. Thought everybody knew.

MARIE. *(From below.)* I don't believe it. *(MARIE climbs up from below.)*

CHARLIE. Shhh.

MARIE. *(In a loud whisper.)* You break into my daughter's home, steal her things, then have a camp-out across the road? Charlie, *he* is supposed to be the senile one.

CHARLIE. Why didn't you tell me dad was the anonymous donor?

MARIE. Shhh. *(She signals that Angus isn't to know.)*

CHARLIE. Why not?

MARIE. That was the condition.

CHARLIE. I know, but why would he do that? Why wouldn't he want Gramp to know?

SPENCER. Prob'ly figured the old fart 'd say no.

CHARLIE. Well he's wrong. *(Goes to wake ANGUS.)*

MARIE. Charlie, don't.

CHARLIE. I'm telling you this will make the difference. Gramp, wake— *(Recoils.)*

MARIE. Oh, God.

SPENCER. Ah man, no. . . . Shit.

A dog barks. MARIE wraps herself in the shawl, transforming into MAE.

MAE. So, old man, you go to meet that cranky old God of yours. . . . You two should get along.

SPENCER. *(Staring down at the form.)* Hey, Charlie . . . thought you said he didn't sign this thing. *(CHARLIE takes it.)*

CHARLIE. "Angus Michael Stewart." *(SPENCER exits.)*

MAE. I tell this story to remind us what we know: that what we care for truly will truly care for us, whether water or sand or children or land. . . . You rest a while, Angus. Then we'll go.

MAE exits. Dog barks. NICK appears in the high loft. He grabs the rope and swings out. HOPLEY's call is heard as lights fade to black.

END OF PLAY

Photograph by Sharon Fosbrook

Charlie and his grandfather Angus in the barn's high loft.

About the Author

Dana Yeaton is the winner of the Heideman Award from the Actors Theatre of Louisville. In addition to *Mad River Rising,* his recent plays include *JUMP CUT,* a one-man video-theatre piece produced at Burlington's Flynn Theatre, and *To Bed with Betsy,* a full-length farce produced at the Volkov Theatre in Yaroslavl, Russia, that country's oldest professional theatre. His dark comedy *Lousy Mothers* was winner of a New Play Fellowship at the Shenandoah International Playwrights Retreat in Virginia.

Yeaton is the author of many plays for young adults, including *Democracy Rules! A Rally for Activism, Garden of Needham,* and *Alice in Love,* winner of the 1993 Vermont State Drama Festival. He has received three fellowships in playwriting from the Vermont Arts Council. Currently he teaches dramatic writing at Middlebury College and is Managing Director of Vermont Stage Company, where he founded the Vermont Young Playwrights Project.

About PenStroke Press

PenStroke Press is a student publishing venture that was initiated at Rochester High School in September of 1997 through a grant from the Randolph Regional School-to-Work Consortium, with additional funding from the Vermont Arts Council Partners-in-Education grant. The press is a partnership project between Rochester High School and two professional publishing companies—Inner Traditions International and Schenkman Books.

PenStroke Press thanks Webcom printing company of Toronto, Canada, a member of the Vermont Book Professionals Association, for their continuing community outreach support, and Castleton State College, which helped to underwrite the cost of printing this book.

An Anthology of Ten-Minute Plays from the Vermont Young Playwrights Project

Blasts from the Future: An Anthology of Ten-Minute Plays from the Vermont Young Playwrights Project

Edited by Dana Yeaton
Foreword by Congressman Bernie Sanders

176 pages, 5 1/4" x 8 1/4"
ISBN 0-9669177-0-7
Paperback
$10.00

Blasts from the Future is, to our knowledge, the very first published anthology of ten-minute plays by middle and high school students. The plays were selected from the first three years of the Vermont Young Playwrights Project—an outreach program of the Vermont Stage Company—which sends professional playwrights into schools throughout the state.

The seventeen plays collected in *Blasts from the Future* represent a vast array of themes and characters—from the serious to the sublime to the truly silly. There is something in *Blasts* for everyone's taste. With small casts and simple or implied settings, they are perfect for productions that are easy to mount or tour.

Blasts from the Future is a production of PenStroke Press and was first published in January of 1999.

To order *Blasts from the Future* contact PenStroke Press at 118 Main Street, Rochester, Vermont 05767 • 802-767-3702 • FAX 802-767-9528 • email schenkma@sover.net.

VERMONT STATE COLLEGES
0 0003 0654773 8